escapism artist

Libby Burnette

BookLeaf Publishing

India | USA | UK

Presentation by *BookLeaf Publishing*

Web: www.bookleafpub.com

E-mail: info@bookleafpub.com

ISBN: 9789358319828

First edition 2023

weedkiller

Give me a weedkiller
for the gardens of my mind
These days I spend the sundowns
on my knees plucking figments
until my fingers ache with yearning
for things that once were;
things that never were;
things that never will

Seasons on seasons pass through
fields that have for years lain fallow
still thoughts of you surface unbidden
like so many stinging nettles

fragile heart

Fragile heart,
take this gentle gift:
pulling your fingers
from where they sit
frozen, carved in stone,
clenched in the tightest fist
Knifelike nails digging crescent
moon-shaped scars - relinquish it.

What good can the clutching do
refusal to release resentment

Those bitter thorns buried, still
they wound with every breath?

anticipation

It's in the breath before you kiss her
quiet, preternatural stillness
speaks only in whispers, then not at all
her lashes hanging low as the moon above

A moment balanced on a knife's edge
sharp and crystalline
before you bend to gravity
as delicate as falling snow

tightrope

You walk a tightrope
strung between the roof
of the house where you were born
and some distant point, obscured
by clouds that smother you

The wire twisting
ever tighter around your lungs
tugs insistently, digs
lines into your heart, fragments
your ribs, leaves the taste
of metal on your tongue
And the sound of wind
whipping past your ears,
blinding sun in your eyes

The air is thin up here
gasping, trembling, paralyzed
vertigo swelling in your stomach
and they tell you to walk faster

Can't they see that
any centimeter's misstep
could send you
plummeting

salt and rust

Do I alarm you
with the magnitude of my affection -
a step ahead, a meter deeper,
always drowning?

Can you taste the words I bite back -
salt and rust
on the tip of my tongue?

"Good night, love,
good morning, love,
thank you, love,"
Endearment spills so casually from your lips,
dangerous to say words you don't mean.

So I will call you any name but that;
I cannot trust the word to escape my mouth
lest the floodgates open forever -

(I love you, I love you, I love you)

And I would give you anything
if you would only ask for it;
would you? ask for it?

between words

In the spaces between words
and in brief flashes
I glimpse your future
weariness
in fearful certainty
For you will be broken
too soon to imagine
and not so far off now

I have seen the shift in you
towards solitary silence
And regret never taking
the chance to call you a friend
Is it too late?

So strange to love, to idolize,
and still to know so little
Superficial boundaries never crossed
through a lifetime of embraces
and a spirit at arm's length
What will I be left with?

And yet I do know you;
I am you, twins in temperament
In our discomfort at being seen

laid bare
we rely on the company of others
for balance, to draw ourselves out
two protons never pull each other close

But I found the yellowed pages
where you drafted words to songs
and when I put them to music
it felt as if I had written them myself

bottle

I wish I could bottle the sounds you make
roll your scent into a cigarette
like it doesn't already constrict my lungs

Lying in the blue satin dark,
frayed at the seams between fear and desire
time drips viscous through my hands

And after you leave
the tender fingers of your ghost
wrap around my throat
and squeeze a little

sycamore

Now I am often plagued
with the twisting of my insides
the type that makes you want
to dig your fingernails into your skin
strip the flesh from your body
rip out your warm, beating heart
and stop feeling
so damn
wretched –

Maybe I will someday stop imagining
how it would feel to harvest my organs
and plant them
so a sycamore sprouts
from the remnants of my lungs

pompeii

The first time you ever saw me
I was singing this song for you
years by your side elapsed
in playlists and concerts and records
that you queued all night to buy

Here lies what once was us:
teary-eyed in a crowded room
a month gone since our empire's fall
scream along, begging for answers

"How am I gonna be an optimist about this?"

dynamic instability

When everything is going
too well, suspiciously smoothly
In comes that old urge
- "upend it all"

Whispering, softly
all we know is striving, we
have no taste for comfort
we get restless

Like a child labors painstakingly
over his tower of blocks, then
knocks them down with glee

catastrophe

simple days

In those simple days
we lay in sunshine like cats
like plants, like wild flowers
in light and laughter and tall grass

Before lightning struck the oak,
in those simple days,
we tied ropes to its branches
and swung in vast parabolas

Carrying secrets like currency,
collecting stones to twist in twine
In those simple days
we lived beyond explanation

And I remember sunflowers
that towered past our heads
protecting us from heat and harm
in those simple days

daydream

You said,
don't let yourself become
so enamored with a daydream
that you self-destruct

But I can't help it; you're the sunshine
bursting through the clouds in my lungs
too brilliant to look at head-on
warming my frostbite hands and heart

You are the sun
and I am Icarus,

flying

falling

small

I forgot how small you made me feel
until you reached out again today
lulled into comfort by the silence

Now waking to your name
an apparition on my screen
brought it crashing back torrents of shivering
shimmering nervousness a knot
deep in my stomach static filling my mind

How did I forget
every time I sat waiting
for your mercurial temper to appear
accusatory, hyper-critical
short of fuse and raised of voice
while I remained thin-skinned in admiration
my best and worst memories
of a year and a half at your hand

In an instant I am again
the creature I once was, insecurity
pulsing through my limbs, fingernails
bitten to the quick, desperately
searching for shelter from the fear
that you will see through me,

knock me off the shelf
label me a fraud. I believed
I had grown but all I can think
is please don't catch me out --

All I wanted was to make you proud.

morning light

Before I ever said the words
I wrote them
in golden sunday strokes,
late morning sunlight streaming
through the blinds
as you lay peaceful, rhythmic rise
and fall of breath I traced
in clusters of languages
lazy lines skimming skin
je t'aime te amo 我愛你
casting spells with my fingers
wishing not to wake you
watching the pattern sink
into the freckles of your back

The first morning I woke wondering
why I had slept so long
as I grew conscious I felt
the warmth next to me, your arm
around my waist and slowly
twisted to see all tension
faded from your face, contented
smile set in the corners of your eyes
and I had to stare for just a moment
overwhelmed at how I got
everything I never dared to ask for

heavy

Sometimes I glimpse
phantom tendrils of my own sorrows
wind themselves around your neck
and drag you down to join me
in the depths of these
caverns of grey matter
And even in your reassurance
it is in these times that I
despise my mind the most
Consumed by cold creeping
into the bones of my chest,
this double bladed knife
afraid that I've come to lean
too much on your comfort, and
afraid that someday -
not today, and maybe not soon -
but someday, you will decide
my heart is too heavy to bear

polaroid

I found an old picture of us last summer
A polaroid, dusty relic of old selves
wearing pleated skirts and quiet smiles, hesitant
on the edge of life

Her deep green eyes, tiger-striped, fluttered
softly shut before she kissed me - I wonder
if she recalls August days? We were fifteen,
restless and reckless

Holding our breath upstairs and out the window
to the roof next door, our hands full of splinters.
nonchalance dripping from her dark, heavy curls
Does she remember?

bishop

I am in love with the land.
The stillness
of the early desert morning
sun already high at seven
the taste of snow in crisp December air,
over sere ground - no clouds
but those you can hardly see
clustered at the white-tipped mountains

The silence, shattered
by the rustle of a million zippers
groans
'morning
eggs eaten blistering hot
straight out of the pot
on a tiny gas stove -
nothing else could ever taste so good

And returning in the pitch black
Stars, like we stuck safety pins
through the velvet atmosphere,
are swallowed by a bonfire built
of wooden pallets stolen
from the kmart parking lot

Friends of friends, sit together, warm the frost
from your bones
sing songs of victory and defeat
comparing your torn skin and calloused scars,
remnants of sisyphean battles against boulders:

Hauling ourselves up by the fingers
til we fall back to earth,
silhouetted by the waning sun

thistle

I cannot pull away from cruelty
I hear my own voice, petty, bratty,
needlessly pedantic, a step too far
to be rightly called playful snark

for I am compelled to throw the worst
of me at you, a challenge, desperately
wishing you to take it in stride

as if I don't believe
that you could possibly want who I am,
the fucked-up brain of this howling creature
dares you into proving it right,
even as it hopes against hope
to be proven wrong

so I build myself a thicket
entomb my heart in thistles
and maybe you will cut through;
maybe you will love the thorns

www.ingramcontent.com/pod-product-compliance
Lightning Source LLC
Chambersburg PA
CBHW071257140726
47996CB00007B/2880